**Another Related Title:**

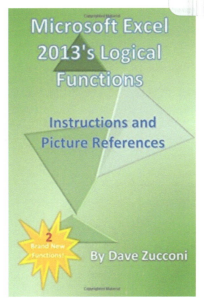

**Covering the following functions:**

And

False

If

IfError

IfNA

Not

Or

True

XOR

**Conveniently available on Amazon!**

www.exceltutorialswithdave.com

# Contents

## About the author

My name is David and I go by Dave. I am 27 years old have a fair amount of irrelevant knowledge about somewhat obscure things. I graduated from the University of Maryland, Baltimore County (UMBC) in 2009 with a BA in Psychology. I have a strong passion for helping people, and Microsoft Excel happens to be a way that I can help many people. I started this adventure in March of 2014, and it has proven to be very rewarding.

You have probably heard the old cliché, "Give a man a fish and he eats for a day, but teach a man to fish and he eats for life". We of course would have to assume that the man could fish far more effectively than I can. Regardless, I believe in the concept that people are best taught to teach themselves. I liken this concept to, "Train the trainer" but I hold nothing but respect for those teaching themselves for personal growth.

I intend to accompany you on your journey, which starts here. I hope that this printed reference guide proves to be helpful and becomes a part of your active desktop collection.

This is your first step. This is a big step. Congratulations, and get ready to unlock your potential with the help of Microsoft Excel!

# Information Functions

## Cell

Why is this function useful?

The Cell function has a great deal of value when you are seeking information about a particular cell. In fact the name of the first argument is "info_type". The information type is predefined so try not to fret. Remember to use this in your formulas where you really would prefer to preform functions on cells that contain certain qualities. The second argument is where you define the cell that you are analyzing. This argument, however, is optional. Should you chose to leave this argument out, the formula will analyze the last cell changed, which will update every time you change a cell.

Take a look at the different predefined information types below:

| info_type | Description | For Example |
|---|---|---|
| address | This will be an absolute reference to the cell address. | Referencing cell A1 you will receive the value "$A$1". |
| col | This will be an integer value of the column referenced. | Referencing cell A1 you will receive the value "1". |
| color | This will be a value of "1" or "0" based on the formatting. "1" where formatting will highlight negative numbers in red, "0" in all other cases. | You MUST select a red highlighted selection from the Number tab in the Format Cells dialog box. Only the Number and Currency categories will have this option. |
| contents | This will be the value of the cell referenced. This will not return a formula. | Referencing a cell containing "=SUM(A:A)" would return an integer representing the results of that formula. |
| filename | If the file has been saved, this will return the entire file path to | Referencing a cell on Sheet1 may return: C:\Excel\[File.xlsx]Sheet1 |

4

| info_type | Description | For Example |
|---|---|---|
| | the cell referenced. | |
| format | This will be a shorthand code that translates to the Number format of the cell. | Referencing a cell with a percentage showing two decimal points will return the value "P2". |
| parentheses | This will be a value of "1" or "0" based on the formatting. "1" where formatting will encapsulate positive numbers in parentheses, "0" in all other cases. | Referencing a cell containing a custom format such as "(General)" the function may return the value "1". |
| prefix | This will indicate the horizontal alignment of your cell text. Note: you will get an empty string if the cell does not contain text. | ' = General, Left, Justify, Distributed<br>^ = Center, Center Across Selection<br>" = Right<br>\ = Fill |
| protect | This will be a value of "1" or "0" based on the cell protection. "1" if the cell is locked, "0" if the cell is not locked. Note: this does not indicate if the sheet is or is not protected. | Referencing a cell that will be locked when a sheet is protected will return the value "1". |
| row | This will be an integer value of the row referenced. | Referencing cell A1 you will receive the value "1". |
| type | This will be one of three values:<br>"b" for a blank cell<br>"v" for a cell containing a numeric value<br>"l" for a cell containing a text label | Referencing a cell containing the integer "45" would return the letter "v". |

| info_type | Description | For Example |
|---|---|---|
| width | This will be the nearest integer value (rounded) of the column width referenced. | Referencing a cell with a 10.49 width would return the value "10". |

How difficult is this function to use?

This function is very easy to use with a caveat noting that the versatile nature of this function makes understanding all of the capabilities more a complex task.

How do I use this function?

1.  Open Microsoft Excel and locate the data that you wish to analyze.

2.  Activate the cell where you want to display the result of your cell evaluation.

3.  Type the Cell function, "=CELL(".

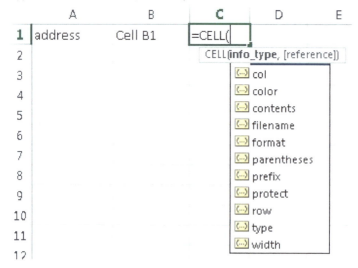

4. Input your first argument, in this example, """address""". This argument is the portion that you define the info_type mentioned in the description.

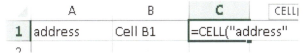

5. If you wish to assign a particular static cell, then type a comma to move to the next argument. For a dynamic cell value, skip to step number 7.

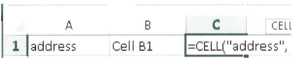

6. Input your next argument, in this example, "B1".

7. Complete the function with a closing parenthesis ")".

8. Hit "Enter".

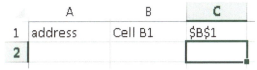

9. Congratulations! You have used the Cell function! Below are examples of each element of the Cell function. The label in column A, value in column B, and the result in column C.

|   | A | B | C | D | E |
|---|---|---|---|---|---|
| 1 | address | Cell B1 | $B$1 | | |
| 2 | col | Cell B2 | 2 | | |
| 3 | color | 5000.00 | 1 | | |
| 4 | contents | Cell B4 | Cell B4 | | |
| 5 | filename | Cell B5 | C:\Excel\[File.xlsx]Sheet1 | | |
| 6 | format | 59.25% P2 | | | |
| 7 | parentheses | (200) | 1 | | |
| 8 | prefix | Cell B8 " | | | |
| 9 | protect | Cell B9 | 1 | | |
| 10 | row | Cell B10 | 10 | | |
| 11 | type | 45 v | | | |
| 12 | width | Cell B12 | 10 | | |

## Error.Type

Why is this function useful?

This function takes the seven error messages in Microsoft Excel and converts them to an integer representing that specific error message. You may have already jumped to this conclusion but this function essentially allows us to create a finite IfError function. No one wants the "#DIV/0!" error message showing up on their spreadsheet, especially customers that lack familiarity with Excel.

But let's say that you may also anticipate a "#N/A" error in the same formula? Now you can begin to define error messages for the different use cases that you find. Now your not-so-savvy users can get (and give you) good information about why the value of your formula was not what they expected. You can show "No denominator" instead of the "#DIV/0!" error as well as "No matching records found" instead of the "#N/A" error.

| Error.Type Value | Generic Error Code |
|---|---|
| #N/A | Anything not otherwise defined. |
| 1 | #NULL! |
| 2 | #DIV/0! |

| Error.Type Value | Generic Error Code |
|---|---|
| 3 | #VALUE! |
| 4 | #REF! |
| 5 | #NAME? |
| 6 | #NUM! |
| 7 | #N/A |
| 8 | #GETTING_DATA |

How difficult is this function to use?

This function is complex to use by the nature of the additional setup it will take to utilize the integers returned in a meaningful way but the formula itself is actually quite easy to enter.

How do I use this function?

1. Open Microsoft Excel and locate the data that you wish to use, most likely an error message.

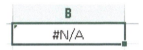

2. Activate the cell where you want to display the result of your Error.Type evaluation.

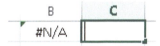

3. Type the Error.Type function, "ERROR.TYPE(".

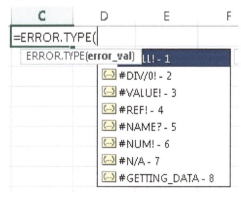

4.  Input the address of the cell you would like to reference, in this example "B1".

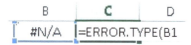

5.  Complete the function with a closing parenthesis ")".

6.  Hit "Enter".

7.  Congratulations!  You have used the Error.Type function!  While this function won't ever be something that will make or break your sheet, it can really help to make your sheets look more professional.

## Info

Why is this function useful?

The Info function in Microsoft Excel gives you a great deal of information that will likely be helpful in troubleshooting problems. What I mean is that there is a great deal of information that you may not know about your machine that you can now easily access thanks to this Excel function.

Have you ever been to a help forum online where you were asked to provide information that you just didn't know how to find or where to look to get it? This likely contains the information that you are looking for concerning anything Excel and maybe even your operating system.

As you become more advanced, this function can also allow you to do things like customize formulas for specific versions of Excel. If a new formula is available in 2013 that you would like to use, but you have some customers still on 2010, then here is where you find out which version the user has on their machine.

Take a look at each of the options for the Info function in Excel 2013 below:

| Information Type | Description |
|---|---|
| directory | The file path containing the active workbook. Note: this does NOT contain the filename. |
| numfile | The number of worksheets in the ALL open workbooks. |
| origin | An absolute reference of the cell at the top left of the screen which is preceded with "$A:". Note: this will change as you scroll through your document. |
| osversion | The version of your current operating system. |
| recalc | The recalculation mode of your workbook. The two possible values are: Automatic Manual |
| release | The version of Microsoft Excel that you are running. |
| system | This will show the name of your operating environment. The two possible values are: pcdos for Windows machines mac for Macintosh machines |

How difficult is this function to use?

This function is very easy to use. This formula is entirely self-contained and does not refer to any information in the spreadsheet.

How do I use this function?

1. Open Microsoft Excel.

2. Activate the cell where you want to display the result of your information evaluation.

3. Type the Info function, "=INFO(".

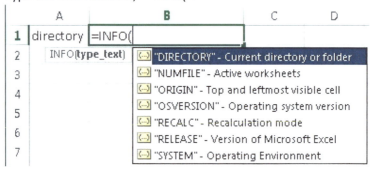

4. Input your argument, in this example, ""directory"". This argument is the portion that you define the information type mentioned in the description.

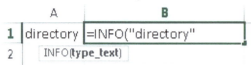

5. Complete the function with a closing parenthesis ")".

6. Hit "Enter".

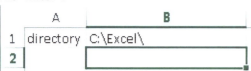

7. Congratulations! You have used the Info function! Below are examples of each element of the Info function. The label in column A, and the result in column B.

www.exceltutorialswithdave.com

| | A | B |
|---|---|---|
| 1 | directory | C:\Excel\ |
| 2 | numfile | 3 |
| 3 | origin | $A:$A$1 |
| 4 | osversion | Windows (64-bit) NT 6.01 |
| 5 | recalc | Automatic |
| 6 | release | 15.0 |
| 7 | system | pcdos |

## IsBlank

Why is this function useful?

This function is useful to determine if a cell truly is blank or if it is not. If you are new to Excel, this may seem like a silly notion. I have been in your shoes and I understand why it would seem that way but I assure you that it is actually quite helpful. Getting a value of "TRUE" for a blank cell or a value of "FALSE" for a cell that is not blank can come in handy.

This function will weed out cells that are obviously not blank as well as the cells that contain only a space character. You may be surprised at how many people will utilized the space bar as if it were the delete key. If you are guilty of it, that is okay. Please don't do that anymore but don't worry about having done it in the past.

Using spaces instead of deleting can cause issues where the developer has issued a trigger based on the cell containing some sort of value. For instance, protecting a division function. I don't want to attempt to divide by a blank value. So I may have set the cell to divide if it finds that the cell in not blank. Now, instead, I may have a formula that attempts to divide by a cell containing no value. It's not the end of the world, the "#DIV/0!" error message should make the point clearly enough. Not to mention that this issue can still be avoided by the developer.

If the developer utilizes the Trim function before evaluating the cell to determine if it is or is not blank, then the space(s) will be removed showing a blank value. Be aware developers: The IsBlank formula will still show false when using the Trim function but you will be able to correctly evaluate a cell reference equal to nothing (eg. A1="").

How difficult is this function to use?

This function is very easy to use.

How do I use this function?

1. Open Microsoft Excel and locate the cell that you wish to evaluate.

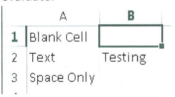

2. Activate the cell where you want to display the result of your logical test.

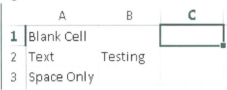

3. Type the IsBlank function, "=ISBLANK(".

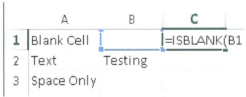

4. Input your first (and only) argument, in this example "B1". This argument should be a reference to a cell. If you input a range, the result will always show "FALSE".

| | A | B | C |
|---|---|---|---|
| 1 | Blank Cell | | =ISBLANK(B1 |
| 2 | Text | Testing | |
| 3 | Space Only | | |

5. Complete the function with a closing parenthesis ")".

| | A | B | C |
|---|---|---|---|
| 1 | Blank Cell | | =ISBLANK(B1) |
| 2 | Text | Testing | |
| 3 | Space Only | | |

6. Hit "Enter".

| | A | B | C |
|---|---|---|---|
| 1 | Blank Cell | | TRUE |
| 2 | Text | Testing | |
| 3 | Space Only | | |

7. Congratulations, you have now successfully used the IsBlank function! Remember that you can use this inside any other function that takes a logical argument. The IsBlank function will return a Boolean value. Below is an example of what happens when you copy that formula down column C using the Fill Handle.

| | A | B | C |
|---|---|---|---|
| 1 | Blank Cell | | TRUE |
| 2 | Text | Testing | FALSE |
| 3 | Space Only | | FALSE |
| 4 | | | |

## IsErr

Why is this function useful?

The IsErr function is helpful any time you will need to determine if there is or is not an error message in one of your cells. Bear in mind that you will not be capturing the "#N/A" error message. Effectively, this function will return the value "TRUE" if there are any of the other error messages or return the value of "FALSE" making it effective for monitoring your spreadsheet for any errors.

I would also like to note that not all error messages mean that you have done anything wrong in producing your spreadsheet. In fact, I mean quite the opposite. Many formulas are designed and tested to contain information in ideal circumstances. When normal operating conditions are interrupted, perhaps a the start of a new year and a brand new "clean" workbook, you are likely to find error messages because your well designed formulas simply don't have the values that are necessary for proper calculation. Annual budget and burn-rate tracking comes to mind for me immediately but think about spreadsheets that you might use in your day-to-day job.

15

Rather than working with a mass amount of possible outcomes, this function will tell you immediately, "TRUE" you have an error (other than "#N/A") or "FALSE" you do not have an error in the referenced cell.

For more information about handling error messages in Microsoft Excel 2013 try checking out the following functions:

| Category | Function Name |
| --- | --- |
| Logical | IfError |
| Logical | IfNA |
| Information | Error.Type |
| Information | IsErr (This Function) |
| Information | IsError |
| Information | IsNA |

How difficult is this function to use?

This function is very easy to use and the simple "TRUE" or "FALSE" format result is easy to interpret.

How do I use this function?

1. Open Microsoft Excel and locate the cell that you wish to evaluate.

2. Activate the cell where you want to display the result of your logical test.

3. Type the IsErr function, "=ISERR(".

4. Input your first (and only) argument, in this example "B1". This argument should be a reference to a cell. If you input a range, the result will always show "TRUE".

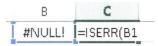

| B | C |
|---|---|
| #NULL! | =ISERR(B1 |

5. Complete the function with a closing parenthesis ")".

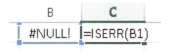

| B | C |
|---|---|
| #NULL! | =ISERR(B1) |

6. Hit "Enter".

| B | C |
|---|---|
| #NULL! | TRUE |

7. Congratulations, you have now successfully used the IsErr function! Remember that you can use this inside any other function that takes a logical argument. The IsErr function will return a Boolean value. Below is an example of what happens when you copy that formula down column C using the Fill Handle.

| | A | B | C |
|---|---|---|---|
| 1 | Error Message | #NULL! | TRUE |
| 2 | Error Message | #DIV/0! | TRUE |
| 3 | Error Message | #VALUE! | TRUE |
| 4 | Error Message | #REF! | TRUE |
| 5 | Error Message | #NAME? | TRUE |
| 6 | Error Message | #NUM! | TRUE |
| 7 | Error Message | #N/A | FALSE |
| 8 | Error Message | #GETTING_DATA | TRUE |
| 9 | Text | This is a text cell | FALSE |
| 10 | Number | 1337 | FALSE |
| 11 | Blank Cell | | FALSE |

## IsError

Why is this function useful?

17

The IsError function will help you to determine if there is or is not an error message in one of your cells. With this function you will be capturing all of the error messages to include the "#N/A" error message. Effectively, this function will return the value "TRUE" if there are any error messages at all or return the value of "FALSE" making it effective for monitoring your spreadsheet for any errors.

Error messages are a common occurrence in advanced Excel spreadsheets and each error is meant to give you information about what is occurring. It will, however, take a little bit of your insight to effectively communicate with or troubleshoot on behalf of your users. Take the presence of an error as an opportunity to refine how your formula reacts to the surrounding stimuli rather than an alert that something is wrong. Take it from me, error messages are all a part of developing an advanced and effective spreadsheet.

Rather than working with a mass amount of possible outcomes, this function will tell you immediately, "TRUE" you have an error (including "#N/A") or "FALSE" you do not have an error in the referenced cell.

For more information about handling error messages in Microsoft Excel 2013 try checking out the following functions:

| Category | Function Name |
|---|---|
| Logical | IfError |
| Logical | IfNA |
| Information | Error.Type |
| Information | IsErr |
| Information | IsError (This Function) |
| Information | IsNA |

How difficult is this function to use?

This function is very easy to use and the simple "TRUE" or "FALSE" format result is easy to interpret.

How do I use this function?

1. Open Microsoft Excel and locate the cell that you wish to evaluate.

2. Activate the cell where you want to display the result of your logical test.

3. Type the IsError function, "=ISERROR(".

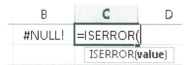

4. Input your first (and only) argument, in this example "B1". This argument should be a reference to a cell. If you input a range, the result will always show "TRUE".

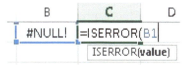

5. Complete the function with a closing parenthesis ")".

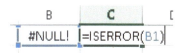

6. Hit "Enter".

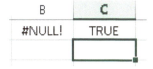

7. Congratulations, you have now successfully used the IsError function! Remember that you can use this inside any other function that takes a logical argument. The IsError function will return a Boolean value. Below is an example of what happens when you copy that formula down column C using the Fill Handle.

|    | A             | B                 | C     |
|----|---------------|-------------------|-------|
| 1  | Error Message | #NULL!            | TRUE  |
| 2  | Error Message | #DIV/0!           | TRUE  |
| 3  | Error Message | #VALUE!           | TRUE  |
| 4  | Error Message | #REF!             | TRUE  |
| 5  | Error Message | #NAME?            | TRUE  |
| 6  | Error Message | #NUM!             | TRUE  |
| 7  | Error Message | #N/A              | TRUE  |
| 8  | Error Message | #GETTING_DATA     | TRUE  |
| 9  | Text          | This is a text cell | FALSE |
| 10 | Number        | 1337              | FALSE |
| 11 | Blank Cell    |                   | FALSE |
| 12 |               |                   |       |

## IsEven

Why is this function useful?

There are many reasons why you might want to determine if a number is or is not even. Thankfully, if a number is not even then it has to be odd so you could use the IsEven or the IsOdd function to accomplish the same task. This is, of course, entirely true! IsEven will return a value of "TRUE" if the number referenced is even or the value of "FALSE" if the number is not even. The two functions simply oppose one another. There are still several interesting facts about these two functions.

Interesting facts about IsEven:

- A blank cell is evaluated as the even number zero.
- Non-numeric references will return the "#VALUE!" error message.
- Decimals (consequently fractions and times as well) are not considered in the logical test. I cannot speak to the design of this function but it appears that the referenced value is being converted to an integer (rounded down) prior to evaluation.
- You can use "NOT(ISODD(A1))" to achieve the same result as "ISEVEN(A1)". You should not do that but I try to get

20

you to continue thinking outside of the box even if sometimes it simply replicates another functionality. This kind of exploration is how new functions are born. Note: there were 51 functions added to Microsoft Excel 2013 compared to Microsoft Excel 2010.

How difficult is this function to use?

This function is very easy to use and the simple "TRUE" or "FALSE" format result is easy to interpret.

How do I use this function?

1. Open Microsoft Excel and locate the cell that you wish to evaluate.

2. Activate the cell where you want to display the result of your logical test.

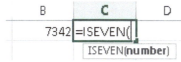

3. Type the IsEven function, "=ISEVEN(".

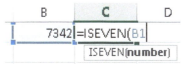

4. Input your first (and only) argument, in this example "B1". This argument should be a reference to a cell. If you input a range, the result will always show "#VALUE!".

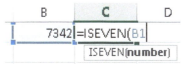

5. Complete the function with a closing parenthesis ")".

6. Hit "Enter".

| | B | C |
|---|---|---|
| | 7342 | TRUE |

7. Congratulations, you have now successfully used the IsEven function! Remember that you can use this inside any other function that takes a logical argument. The IsEven function will return a Boolean value. Below is an example of what happens when you copy that formula down column C using the Fill Handle.

| | A | B | C |
|---|---|---|---|
| 1 | Even Number | 7342 | TRUE |
| 2 | Odd Number | 1337 | FALSE |
| 3 | Decemial | 7342.5 | TRUE |
| 4 | Date | 4/1/2015 | FALSE |
| 5 | Date and Time | 4/1/2015 12:00 PM | FALSE |
| 6 | Fraction | 7342 1/2 | TRUE |
| 7 | Text | This is text | #VALUE! |
| 8 | | | |

## IsFormula

Why is this function useful?

The IsFormula function was added to Microsoft Excel 2013 and just like the name implies, it helps users to determine if there is or is not a formula in the cell referenced. The formula will return the value "TRUE" if there is a formula and will return the value of "FALSE" if there is not a formula.

I think the utility of this function is pretty clear to those of us that have ever been in the situation where we could have used it but to those that have not, this function tends to seem unnecessary. Considering how easy it would be to click on a cell and to look at the Function Bar to determine if there is or is not a function this almost seems silly. I understand why you might feel that way but trust me, there are many reasons to implement this function as you work in Excel.

I tend to use this function in two scenarios.

The first and most common scenario is when I distribute a spreadsheet containing formulas, and my customer complains that the functionality is no longer working automatically. Rather than click on 1000 rows and look at the Function Bar, I will use this function to copy down an adjacent/empty column.

The second scenario is less common but results in a more critical need for this formula. When I receive a protected spreadsheet and I cannot predict cells that are supposed to update automatically. Even protected cells can be referenced using the IsFormula function.

Don't forget to consider the possibility of utilizing the Boolean results of this formula in a more functional evaluation if it might be useful to you. Grab a copy of our publication "Microsoft Excel 2013's Logical Functions" if you would like to know more about the Logical Functions in Microsoft Excel.

How difficult is this function to use?

This function is very easy to use and the simple "TRUE" or "FALSE" format result is easy to interpret.

How do I use this function?

1. Open Microsoft Excel and locate the data that you wish to evaluate.

|   | A | B |
|---|---|---|
| 1 | 26 |  |
| 2 | 15 |  |

2. Activate the cell where you want to display the result of your logical test.

|   | A | B |
|---|---|---|
| 1 | 26 |  |
| 2 | 15 |  |

3. Type the IsFormula function, "=ISFORMULA(".

4. Input your first (and only) argument, in this example "A1". This argument should be a reference to a cell. If you input a range, the top-left most cell will be evaluated.

5. Complete the function with a closing parenthesis ")".

6. Hit "Enter".

7. Congratulations, you have now successfully used the IsFormula function! Remember that you can use this inside any other function that takes a logical argument. The IsFormula function will return a Boolean value. Below is an example of what happens when you copy that formula down column B using the Fill Handle.

## IsLogical

Why is this function useful?

Quite possibly my favorite function in Microsoft Excel 2013 is the IsLogical function. Admittedly, I don't reach into my bag of tricks to pull this function out frequently but the nature of it really speaks to a guy like

24

me. I can see the humor in a function that will return the value of "TRUE" if it finds either "TRUE" or "FALSE". Conversely, if there is anything else in the referenced cell, this function will return the value of "FALSE".

Despite my terrible sense of humor, this function is incredibly helpful for folks that might be new to programmatic concepts. For instance, you might struggle with a formula which contains some kind of logical test like the If function. Something is wrong and you just can't quite figure out what it could be. Well, the If function requires the first argument to be "TRUE" or "FALSE". In other words, the first argument of an If function must be logical. You can replicate that argument in the IsLogical function to determine if the result is or is not considered logical.

You may be familiar with the True and the False Logical functions in Excel 2013. You may also realize that Excel will evaluate many things as logical. For example, the value of zero is considered to be "FALSE" while all other numeric values are considered to be "TRUE". The IsLogical function will not consider these values to be logical. So while your formula may still react the way that you anticipate, the value is not truly logical and will yield a response of "FALSE" from the IsLogical function.

How difficult is this function to use?

This function is very easy to use and the simple "TRUE" or "FALSE" format result is easy to interpret.

How do I use this function?

1. Open Microsoft Excel and locate the cell that you wish to evaluate.

2. Activate the cell where you want to display the result of your logical test.

| B | C |
|---|---|
| TRUE | |

3. Type the IsLogical function, "=ISLOGICAL(".

4. Input your first (and only) argument, in this example "B1". This argument should be a reference to a cell. If you input a range, the result will always show "FALSE".

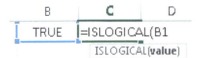

5. Complete the function with a closing parenthesis ")".

6. Hit "Enter".

7. Congratulations, you have now successfully used the IsLogical function! Remember that you can use this inside any other function that takes a logical argument. The IsLogical function will return a Boolean value. Below is an example of what happens when you copy that formula down column C using the Fill Handle.

| | A | B | C |
|---|---|---|---|
| 1 | Logical Statement | TRUE | TRUE |
| 2 | Logical Statement | FALSE | TRUE |
| 3 | Numeric Representation of Logical TRUE | 1 | FALSE |
| 4 | Numeric Representation of Logical FALSE | 0 | FALSE |

## IsNA

Why is this function useful?

The IsNA function is an important counterpart to the IsErr function and can be helpful in identifying the specific "#N/A" error message. Like the IsErr function, the IsNA function will result in only one of two values, "TRUE" or "FALSE". If the value of your referenced cell is

26

"#N/A" then the result will yield "TRUE". If the value of your referenced cell is anything else, to include any other error message then the result will yield "FALSE".

You might also realize that the IsError function is also closely related to the IsNA function. Great! You would be correct. So why would we have two functions (IsNA and IsErr) that we would then need to pair together to capture what it would only take one function (IsError) to accomplish? That is also a great question and it tells me that you are really thinking about the material provided. My response would be two fold. Firstly, get creative. Excel is full of exceptional flexibility that I want to describe to you but the possibilities are just too vast. Secondly, using IsNA and IsErr in concert allows you to handle both cases differently where IsError would handle all error messages the same way.

So why couldn't we pair together IsError and Error.Type to handle different error messages differently? You absolutely can! If you are going to go through the effort of defining what to do in the event of every Error.Type then IsError can actually be taken out of the formula entirely. The world of handling error messages has many options and a great deal of flexibility as I think you are beginning to see.

For more information about handling error messages in Microsoft Excel 2013 try checking out the following functions:

| Category | Function Name |
|---|---|
| Logical | IfError |
| Logical | IfNA |
| Information | Error.Type |
| Information | IsErr |
| Information | IsError |
| Information | IsNA (This Function) |

How difficult is this function to use?

This function is very easy to use and the simple "TRUE" or "FALSE" format result is easy to interpret.

How do I use this function?

1. Open Microsoft Excel and locate the cell that you wish to evaluate.

2. Activate the cell where you want to display the result of your logical test.

3. Type the IsNA function, "=ISNA(".

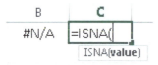

4. Input your first (and only) argument, in this example "B1". This argument should be a reference to a cell. If you input a range, the result will always show "FALSE".

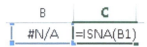

5. Complete the function with a closing parenthesis ")".

6. Hit "Enter".

| B | C |
|------|------|
| #N/A | TRUE |
|  |  |

7. Congratulations, you have now successfully used the IsNA function! Remember that you can use this inside any other function that takes a logical argument. The IsNA function will return a Boolean value. Below is an example of what happens when you copy that formula down column C using the Fill Handle.

| | A | B | C |
|---|---|---|---|
| 1 | Error Message | #NULL! | FALSE |
| 2 | Error Message | #DIV/0! | FALSE |
| 3 | Error Message | #VALUE! | FALSE |
| 4 | Error Message | #REF! | FALSE |
| 5 | Error Message | #NAME? | FALSE |
| 6 | Error Message | #NUM! | FALSE |
| 7 | Error Message | #N/A | TRUE |
| 8 | Error Message | #GETTING_DATA | FALSE |
| 9 | Text | This is a text cell | FALSE |
| 10 | Number | 1337 | FALSE |
| 11 | Blank Cell | | FALSE |
| 12 | | | |

## IsNonText

Why is this function useful?

The IsNonText function is the counterpart to the IsText function and will help you to evaluate if the referenced value is or is not text. IsNonText will return the value of "TRUE" if the value referenced is numeric, or if the cell is blank, and the value of "FALSE" if the value referenced is text or non-numeric symbols like brackets.

This function will also discriminate between formats. What I mean by that is numbers formatted as General, Number, or Percentage will be evaluated as "TRUE" by the IsNonText function. If the number is formatted as Text then the IsNonText function will return the value of "FALSE".

Consider the scenario where your function requires the use of a numeric value or a blank cell. The IsNonText function would be perfect to evaluate the validity of the cell prior to attempting your calculation. Think of this as using an If function to stop and make sure the input elsewhere is valid prior to advancing in the process. At that point you can define what to do next depending on the results.

How difficult is this function to use?

29

This function is very easy to use and the simple "TRUE" or "FALSE" format result is easy to interpret.

How do I use this function?

1. Open Microsoft Excel and locate the cell that you wish to evaluate.

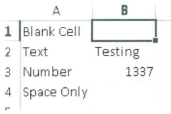

2. Activate the cell where you want to display the result of your logical test.

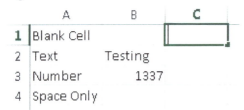

3. Type the IsNonText function, "=ISNONTEXT(".

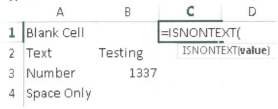

4. Input your first (and only) argument, in this example "B1". This argument should be a reference to a cell. If you input a range, the result will always show "TRUE".

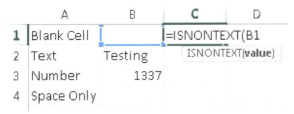

5. Complete the function with a closing parenthesis ")".

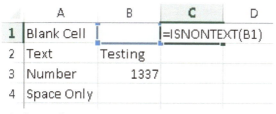

| | A | B | C | D |
|---|---|---|---|---|
| 1 | Blank Cell | | =ISNONTEXT(B1) | |
| 2 | Text | Testing | | |
| 3 | Number | 1337 | | |
| 4 | Space Only | | | |

6. Hit "Enter".

| | A | B | C |
|---|---|---|---|
| 1 | Blank Cell | | TRUE |
| 2 | Text | Testing | |
| 3 | Number | 1337 | |
| 4 | Space Only | | |

7. Congratulations, you have now successfully used the IsNonText function! Remember that you can use this inside any other function that takes a logical argument. The IsNonText function will return a Boolean value. Below is an example of what happens when you copy that formula down column C using the Fill Handle.

| | A | B | C |
|---|---|---|---|
| 1 | Blank Cell | | TRUE |
| 2 | Text | Testing | FALSE |
| 3 | Number | 1337 | TRUE |
| 4 | Space Only | | FALSE |
| 5 | | | |

## IsNumber
Why is this function useful?

The IsNumber function is very similar to the IsNonNumber function and will help you to evaluate if the referenced value is or is not a number. IsNumber will return the value of "TRUE" if the value referenced is numeric and the value of "FALSE" if the value referenced is text, a blank cell, or non-numeric symbols like brackets.

This function will also discriminate between formats. What I mean by that is numbers formatted as General, Number, or Percentage will be evaluated as "TRUE" by the IsNumber function. If the number is

31

formatted as Text then the IsNumber function will return the value of "FALSE".

Consider the scenario where your function requires the use of a numeric value. The IsNumber function would be perfect to evaluate the validity of the cell prior to attempting your calculation. Think of this as using an If function to stop and make sure the input elsewhere is valid prior to advancing in the process. At that point you can define what to do next depending on the results.

How difficult is this function to use?

This function is very easy to use and the simple "TRUE" or "FALSE" format result is easy to interpret.

How do I use this function?

1. Open Microsoft Excel and locate the cell that you wish to evaluate.

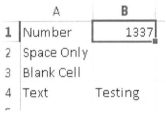

2. Activate the cell where you want to display the result of your logical test.

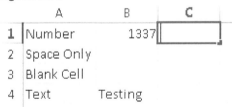

3. Type the IsNumber function, "=ISNUMBER(".

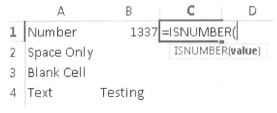

4. Input your first (and only) argument, in this example "B1". This argument should be a reference to a cell. If you input a range, the result will always show "FALSE".

| | A | B | C | D |
|---|---|---|---|---|
| 1 | Number | 1337 | =ISNUMBER(B1 | |
| 2 | Space Only | | ISNUMBER(**value**) | |
| 3 | Blank Cell | | | |
| 4 | Text | Testing | | |

5. Complete the function with a closing parenthesis ")".

| | A | B | C | D |
|---|---|---|---|---|
| 1 | Number | 1337 | =ISNUMBER(B1) | |
| 2 | Space Only | | | |
| 3 | Blank Cell | | | |
| 4 | Text | Testing | | |

6. Hit "Enter".

| | A | B | C |
|---|---|---|---|
| 1 | Number | 1337 | TRUE |
| 2 | Space Only | | |
| 3 | Blank Cell | | |
| 4 | Text | Testing | |

7. Congratulations, you have now successfully used the IsNumber function! Remember that you can use this inside any other function that takes a logical argument. The IsNumber function will return a Boolean value. Below is an example of what happens when you copy that formula down column C using the Fill Handle.

| | A | B | C | |
|---|---|---|---|---|
| 1 | Number | 1337 | TRUE | |
| 2 | Space Only | | FALSE | |
| 3 | Blank Cell | | FALSE | |
| 4 | Text | Testing | FALSE | |
| 5 | | | | |

# IsOdd

Why is this function useful?

There are many reasons why you might want to determine if a number is or is not odd. Thankfully, if a number is not odd then it has to be even so you could use the IsOdd or the IsEven function to accomplish the same task. This is, of course, entirely true! IsOdd will return a value of "TRUE" if the number referenced is odd or the value of "FALSE" if the number is not odd. The two functions simply oppose one another. There are still several interesting facts about these two functions.

Interesting facts about IsOdd:

- A blank cell is evaluated as the even number zero.
- Non-numeric references will return the "#VALUE!" error message.
- Decimals (consequently fractions and times as well) are not considered in the logical test. I cannot speak to the design of this function but it appears that the referenced value is being converted to an integer (rounded down) prior to evaluation.
- You can use "NOT(ISEVEN(A1))" to achieve the same result as "ISODD(A1)". You should not do that but I try to get you to continue thinking outside of the box even if sometimes it simply replicates another functionality. This kind of exploration is how new functions are born. Note: there were 51 functions added to Microsoft Excel 2013 compared to Microsoft Excel 2010.

How difficult is this function to use?

This function is very easy to use and the simple "TRUE" or "FALSE" format result is easy to interpret.

How do I use this function?

1. Open Microsoft Excel and locate the cell that you wish to evaluate.

| B |
|---|
| 1337 |

2. Activate the cell where you want to display the result of your logical test.

3. Type the IsOdd function, "=ISODD(".

4. Input your first (and only) argument, in this example "B1". This argument should be a reference to a cell. If you input a range, the result will always show "#VALUE!".

| B | C | D |
|---|---|---|
| 1337 | =ISODD(B1 | |
| | ISODD(number) | |

5. Complete the function with a closing parenthesis ")".

| B | C |
|---|---|
| 1337 | =ISODD(B1) |

6. Hit "Enter".

| B | C |
|---|---|
| 1337 | TRUE |
| | |

7. Congratulations, you have now successfully used the IsOdd function! Remember that you can use this inside any other function that takes a logical argument. The IsOdd function will return a Boolean value. Below is an example of what happens when you copy that formula down column C using the Fill Handle.

| | A | B | C |
|---|---|---|---|
| 1 | Odd Number | 1337 | TRUE |
| 2 | Even Number | 7342 | FALSE |
| 3 | Decemial | 1337.5 | TRUE |
| 4 | Date | 4/1/2015 | TRUE |
| 5 | Date and Time | 4/1/2015 12:00 PM | TRUE |
| 6 | Fraction | 1337 1/2 | TRUE |
| 7 | Text | This is text | #VALUE! |
| 8 | | | |

## IsRef

Why is this function useful?

IsRef determines if the entered value is a valid reference or if it is not a valid reference. The one, and only, argument for this function should be a cell, range, or named reference. You should never use static values which includes using quotation marks to type out strings of text.

Be aware that this function is not evaluating what the reference contains, rather that the reference is a valid one. This means that A1 might be a valid reference even if the value contained within A1 is actually an error. Otherwise, this function is very straightforward to use.

I like the idea with this function of testing and debugging scalability in your spreadsheet formulas. It also makes quick work of determining if you are spelling a named item correctly or if your formula is simply incorrect. Keep in mind that Microsoft Excel 2013 is limited to 1,048,576 rows and 16,384 columns. Most of you will never reach that or even get close, but some of you just might.

It might also be nice to use this function to first test your references in a longer formula. I don't see that being a practical step, or maybe I am thinking of poor examples. Regardless, I think that particular application of the IsRef function can be avoided by better design of your logical formulas.

How difficult is this function to use?

This function is very easy to use and the simple "TRUE" or "FALSE" format result is easy to interpret.

How do I use this function?

1.  Open Microsoft Excel and locate the information that you wish to evaluate.

|   | A | B |
|---|---|---|
| 1 | Valid Cell | ISREF(A1) |
| 2 | Too Many Rows | ISREF(A1000000000) |
| 3 | Valid Named Range | ISREF(myRange) |
| 4 | Invalid Named Range | =ISREF(noRange) |

2. Activate the cell where you want to display the result of your logical test.

|   | A | B | C |
|---|---|---|---|
| 1 | Valid Cell | ISREF(A1) | |
| 2 | Too Many Rows | ISREF(A1000000000) | |
| 3 | Valid Named Range | ISREF(myRange) | |
| 4 | Invalid Named Range | =ISREF(noRange) | |

3. Type the IsRef function, "=ISREF(".

|   | A | B | C |
|---|---|---|---|
| 1 | Valid Cell | ISREF(A1) | =ISREF( |
| 2 | Too Many Rows | ISREF(A1000000000) | ISREF(**value**) |
| 3 | Valid Named Range | ISREF(myRange) | |
| 4 | Invalid Named Range | =ISREF(noRange) | |

4. Input your first (and only) argument, in this example "A1".

|   | A | B | C |
|---|---|---|---|
| 1 | Valid Cell | ISREF(A1) | =ISREF(A1 |
| 2 | Too Many Rows | ISREF(A1000000000) | ISREF(**value**) |
| 3 | Valid Named Range | ISREF(myRange) | |
| 4 | Invalid Named Range | =ISREF(noRange) | |

5. Complete the function with a closing parenthesis ")".

|   | A | B | C |
|---|---|---|---|
| 1 | Valid Cell | ISREF(A1) | =ISREF(A1) |
| 2 | Too Many Rows | ISREF(A1000000000) | |
| 3 | Valid Named Range | ISREF(myRange) | |
| 4 | Invalid Named Range | =ISREF(noRange) | |

6. Hit "Enter".

| | A | B | C |
|---|---|---|---|
| 1 | Valid Cell | ISREF(A1) | TRUE |
| 2 | Too Many Rows | ISREF(A1000000000) | |
| 3 | Valid Named Range | ISREF(myRange) | |
| 4 | Invalid Named Range | =ISREF(noRange) | |

7. Congratulations, you have now successfully used the IsRef function! The IsRef function will return a Boolean value. Below is an example of what happens when you use each of the formulas displayed below.

| | A | B | C |
|---|---|---|---|
| 1 | Valid Cell | ISREF(A1) | TRUE |
| 2 | Too Many Rows | ISREF(A1000000000) | FALSE |
| 3 | Valid Named Range | ISREF(myRange) | TRUE |
| 4 | Invalid Named Range | =ISREF(noRange) | FALSE |

## IsText

Why is this function useful?

The IsText function is the counterpart to the IsNonText function and will help you to evaluate if the referenced value is or is not text. IsText will return the value of "TRUE" if the value referenced is text, or non-numeric symbols like brackets, and the value of "FALSE" if the value referenced is numeric, or if the cell is blank.

This function will also discriminate between formats. What I mean by that is numbers formatted as General, Number, or Percentage will be evaluated as "FALSE" by the IsText function. If the number is formatted as Text then the IsText function will return the value of "TRUE".

Consider the scenario where your function requires the use of a text value and numeric values wouldn't really make sense. The IsText function would be perfect to evaluate the validity of the cell prior to attempting your calculation. Think of this as using an If function to stop and make sure the input elsewhere is valid prior to advancing in the process. At that point you can define what to do next depending on the results.

How difficult is this function to use?

This function is very easy to use and the simple "TRUE" or "FALSE" format result is easy to interpret.

How do I use this function?

1.  Open Microsoft Excel and locate the cell that you wish to evaluate.

    |   | A | B |
    |---|---|---|
    | 1 | Text | Testing |
    | 2 | Number | 1337 |
    | 3 | Space Only | |
    | 4 | Blank Cell | |

2.  Activate the cell where you want to display the result of your logical test.

    |   | A | B | C |
    |---|---|---|---|
    | 1 | Text | Testing | |
    | 2 | Number | 1337 | |
    | 3 | Space Only | | |
    | 4 | Blank Cell | | |

3.  Type the IsText function, "=ISTEXT(".

    |   | A | B | C |
    |---|---|---|---|
    | 1 | Text | Testing | =ISTEXT( |
    | 2 | Number | 1337 | ISTEXT(**value**) |
    | 3 | Space Only | | |
    | 4 | Blank Cell | | |

4.  Input your first (and only) argument, in this example "B1". This argument should be a reference to a cell. If you input a range, the result will always show "FALSE".

    |   | A | B | C | C |
    |---|---|---|---|---|
    | 1 | Text | Testing | =ISTEXT(B1 | |
    | 2 | Number | 1337 | ISTEXT(**value**) | |
    | 3 | Space Only | | | |
    | 4 | Blank Cell | | | |

5.  Complete the function with a closing parenthesis ")".

39

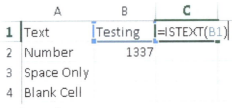

6. Hit "Enter".

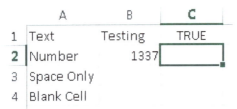

7. Congratulations, you have now successfully used the IsText function! Remember that you can use this inside any other function that takes a logical argument. The IsText function will return a Boolean value. Below is an example of what happens when you copy that formula down column C using the Fill Handle.

|   | A | B | C |
|---|---|---|---|
| 1 | Text | Testing | TRUE |
| 2 | Number | 1337 | FALSE |
| 3 | Space Only |  | TRUE |
| 4 | Blank Cell |  | FALSE |
| 5 |  |  |  |

## N

Why is this function useful?

The N function will convert the referenced value into a numeric value if possible. This is particularly helpful when using functions that require a numeric value. It will eliminate the possibility of getting an error message due to text values. But be warned, text values are returned as the value of zero when using the N function.

Returning the value of zero is scary for several reasons. First, unlike the example below, you will typically not see the result of the directly so if someone slips the letter "O" in instead of the number zero in "1,00O" then you may not recognize the problem right away. Second, zeros are not always that helpful for formulas either. Have you ever tried dividing by zero? Even if a zero slips into a multiplication problem then you can end up with some very strange or unexpected behavior on your spreadsheet.

That being said, the N function is great for getting the numeric representation of dates, times, and Boolean values like true and false. "TRUE" will be "1" and "FALSE" will be "0".

How difficult is this function to use?

This function is moderately difficult to use due to the nature of finding the right time to use this function in a valuable way. I would also like to acknowledge the difficulty in finding valuable help by searching the web for the letter "N". Great for remembering the function itself, but not as helpful when searching.

How do I use this function?

1. Open Microsoft Excel and locate the cell that you wish to evaluate.

| | A | B |
|---|---|---|
| 1 | Time | 7:00 AM |
| 2 | Date | 4/1/2015 |
| 3 | Text | Testing |
| 4 | Number | 1337 |
| 5 | Space Only | |
| 6 | Blank Cell | |
| 7 | Boolean True | TRUE |
| 8 | Boolean False | FALSE |

2. Activate the cell where you want to display the numeric result.

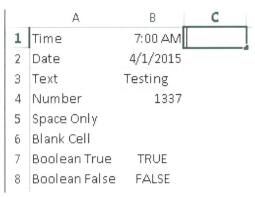

3. Type the N function, "=N(".

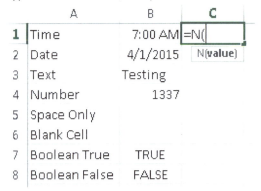

4. Input your first (and only) argument, in this example "B1". This argument should be a reference to a cell. If you input a range, the result will always be an evaluation of the top left most cell in the range.

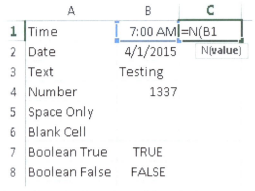

5. Complete the function with a closing parenthesis ")".

| | A | B | C |
|---|---|---|---|
| 1 | Time | 7:00 AM | =N(B1) |
| 2 | Date | 4/1/2015 | |
| 3 | Text | Testing | |
| 4 | Number | 1337 | |
| 5 | Space Only | | |
| 6 | Blank Cell | | |
| 7 | Boolean True | TRUE | |
| 8 | Boolean False | FALSE | |

6.  Hit "Enter".

| | A | B | C |
|---|---|---|---|
| 1 | Time | 7:00 AM | 0.291667 |
| 2 | Date | 4/1/2015 | |
| 3 | Text | Testing | |
| 4 | Number | 1337 | |
| 5 | Space Only | | |
| 6 | Blank Cell | | |
| 7 | Boolean True | TRUE | |
| 8 | Boolean False | FALSE | |

7.  Congratulations, you have now successfully used the N function!
    The N function will return a numeric value. Below is an example of
    what happens when you copy that formula down column C using
    the Fill Handle.

| | A | B | C | D |
|---|---|---|---|---|
| 1 | Time | 7:00 AM | 0.291667 | |
| 2 | Date | 4/1/2015 | 42095 | |
| 3 | Text | Testing | 0 | |
| 4 | Number | 1337 | 1337 | |
| 5 | Space Only | | 0 | |
| 6 | Blank Cell | | 0 | |
| 7 | Boolean True | TRUE | 1 | |
| 8 | Boolean False | FALSE | 0 | |
| 9 | | | | |

## NA

Why is this function useful?

The NA function takes no arguments and returns the text of the NA error message which is "#N/A". The prospect of having a function to do nothing but generate an error message of "Not Applicable" is almost laughable on the surface. If this is your entire formula, you are not accomplishing anything. If you are, however, using this function as part of a larger formula then it can have much more utility.

The value stems from how you are utilizing the error messages within your spreadsheet. Consider for a moment that we have an If function that analyzes a value if the condition is true and the analysis is not applicable if the condition is false. If you intend on handling the errors using something like the IfNA function or even counting the number of errors using a CountIf function then by all means, make sure that you are using the NA function to ensure proper functionality throughout your spreadsheet. If you do not intend on handling the errors in any particular way then your users would likely find more value, and less panic, in the string value of "Not Applicable".

How difficult is this function to use?

This function is moderately difficult to use due to the nature of finding the right time to use this function in a valuable way.

How do I use this function?

1. Open Microsoft Excel and locate the cell where you wish to have the "#N/A" error message displayed.

2. Activate the cell.

3. Type the NA function, "=NA()".

    | A |
    |---|
    | =NA() |

4. Hit "Enter".

5. Congratulations, you have now successfully used the NA function! The NA function will return the "#N/A" error message.

## Sheet

Why is this function useful?

The Sheet function helps you to understand where you are in the order of worksheets in your Excel workbook. It is okay if you didn't follow that. Keep reading. Some of your workbooks will have countless tabs. In fact, according to Microsoft, the number of sheets that you can have in a single workbook is limited only by the available memory that you have. So when you lose your place, it can be helpful to reset your bearings. In smaller workbooks, you can also easily identify if there are hidden worksheets by using this function on the last sheet and determining if the number matches the number of visible sheets. For my more technical audience, this function will also count sheets that are "Very Hidden".

More than resetting your bearings, you can also find the sheet number of Named Ranges, Tables, and worksheets by name. One caveat, the named object must have a scope that makes it available to the entire workbook or you will receive a "#NAME?" error message. Typically the scope is the Workbook on a defined named range, but you can investigate further on the Formula menu by selecting the button labeled "Name Manager". It is not within the scope of this item to describe the Name Manager but I strongly urge you to check it out if you intend to create a large project in Microsoft Excel.

Named Ranges and Tables can be added to this function in the first and only argument, which is optional, without quotation marks. Named Range names can be found in the Name Manager discussed above and the Table name can be found by clicking on a cell within the table and finding the Table Name section in the contextual Design menu which should be activated by default.

Sheet names must be encased within quotation marks. If you fail to use the quotation marks then you will receive a "#NAME?" error.

Let's not forget that the one and only argument is optional. So what happens when you leave the parentheses blank? The function will bring back the number of the sheet that you are currently on.

How difficult is this function to use?

This function is moderately difficult to use because the results of the function can be difficult to understand for users that are not familiar with the function. I would like to point out that the function should be easy to use for those that understand the results.

How do I use this function?

1. Open Microsoft Excel and locate the information that you wish to evaluate.

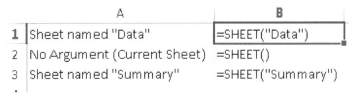

2. Activate the cell where you want to display the numeric result.

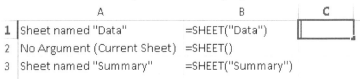

3. Type the Sheet function, "=SHEET(".

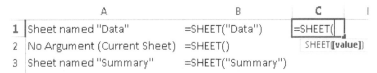

4. Input your first (and only) argument if you wish to do so. This example will have one but having none is more common. The argument should be a sheet name, in this example "Data".

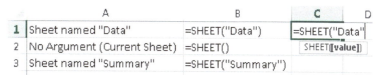

|   | A | B | C | D |
|---|---|---|---|---|
| 1 | Sheet named "Data" | =SHEET("Data") | =SHEET("Data" | |
| 2 | No Argument (Current Sheet) | =SHEET() | SHEET([value]) | |
| 3 | Sheet named "Summary" | =SHEET("Summary") | | |

5.   Complete the function with a closing parenthesis ")".

|   | A | B | C | D |
|---|---|---|---|---|
| 1 | Sheet named "Data" | =SHEET("Data") | =SHEET("Data") | |
| 2 | No Argument (Current Sheet) | =SHEET() | | |
| 3 | Sheet named "Summary" | =SHEET("Summary") | | |

6.   Hit "Enter".

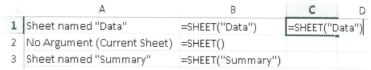

|   | A | B | C |
|---|---|---|---|
| 1 | Sheet named "Data" | =SHEET("Data") | 2 |
| 2 | No Argument (Current Sheet) | =SHEET() | |
| 3 | Sheet named "Summary" | =SHEET("Summary") | |

7.   Congratulations, you have now successfully used the Sheet function! The Sheet function will return a numeric value. Below is an example of what happens when you use each of the formulas displayed below.

|   | A | B | C |
|---|---|---|---|
| 1 | Sheet named "Data" | =SHEET("Data") | 2 |
| 2 | No Argument (Current Sheet) | =SHEET() | 3 |
| 3 | Sheet named "Summary" | =SHEET("Summary") | 1 |

## Sheets

Why is this function useful?

The Sheets function is incredibly helpful for those that understand the function. The Sheets function has one optional argument. If you choose not to add that argument then you will get back a count of the worksheets in the current workbook. The argument itself should be a three dimensional (3D) reference and will return a count of the worksheets included within that 3D reference.

If you are unclear on why this function is so helpful then I assume you could use a quick overview of 3D references and how Microsoft Excel 2013 handles them.

A 3D reference will refer to the same cell address or range over multiple worksheets. In very much the same way that you change a cell reference into a range, you can change a sheet reference into a 3D reference. Add a colon. "Sheet1!A1" refers to one instance of cell A1 but "Sheet1:Sheet3!A1" will refer to three instances of cell A1. However, if you drag Sheet2 outside of that range then you will now only capture two instances. Which means that even your named 3D references are pretty dynamic and susceptible to change if users modify the workbook.

By using a 3D reference by the name "a3DRef" you can continuously validate that it refers to the proper number of sheets using the formula "=SHEETS(a3DRef)". When users reorder the sheets and inadvertently remove a sheet from your defined range, you can give them immediate feedback.

How difficult is this function to use?

This function is complex to use because the results of the function can be difficult to understand for users that are not familiar with the function, and 3D references are not easy to grasp for those that are not savvy.

How do I use this function?

1. Open Microsoft Excel and locate the information that you wish to evaluate.

| | A | B |
|---|---|---|
| 1 | 3D Reference | =SHEETS(a3DRef) |
| 2 | No Argument | =SHEETS() |

2. Activate the cell where you want to display the numeric result.

| | A | B | C |
|---|---|---|---|
| 1 | 3D Reference | =SHEETS(a3DRef) | |
| 2 | No Argument | =SHEETS() | |

3. Type the Sheets function, "=SHEETS(".

| | A | B | C | D |
|---|---|---|---|---|
| 1 | 3D Reference | =SHEETS(a3DRef) | =SHEETS( | |
| 2 | No Argument | =SHEETS() | SHEETS([reference]) | |

48

4.  Input your first (and only) argument if you wish to do so. This example will have one but having none is more common. The argument should be a 3D reference name, in this example "a3DRef".

| | A | B | C | D |
|---|---|---|---|---|
| 1 | 3D Reference | =SHEETS(a3DRef) | =SHEETS(a3DRef | |
| 2 | No Argument | =SHEETS() | SHEETS([reference]) | |

5.  Complete the function with a closing parenthesis ")".

| | A | B | C | D |
|---|---|---|---|---|
| 1 | 3D Reference | =SHEETS(a3DRef) | =SHEETS(a3DRef) | |
| 2 | No Argument | =SHEETS() | | |

6.  Hit "Enter".

| | A | B | C |
|---|---|---|---|
| 1 | 3D Reference | =SHEETS(a3DRef) | 2 |
| 2 | No Argument | =SHEETS() | |

7.  Congratulations, you have now successfully used the Sheets function! The Sheets function will return a numeric value. Below is an example of what happens when you use both of the formulas displayed.

| | A | B | C |
|---|---|---|---|
| 1 | 3D Reference | =SHEETS(a3DRef) | 2 |
| 2 | No Argument | =SHEETS() | 3 |

## Type

Why is this function useful?

The Type function returns an integer based on the type of value in the reference given. The Type function takes only one required argument. The argument can be a value typed directly into the formula or it can be a cell reference. If you choose to refer to a cell, it will evaluate the value in that cell as if it were typed directly into the formula. NOTE: Arrays are not as straightforward as other types.

Consider an instance where users are occasionally motivated to input values in different formats or where you might be forced to handle input in different formats. That is when the Type function can become very useful. You can use this function to handle integers but also determine if text, logical values, or an array is there and handle each of those differently. As a bonus, you can even use this function to determine if the reference contains an error value so that you can decide to handle that differently within this function itself. So you can really slide the scale at which you handle errors, or would be errors, and give your users very detailed and descriptive feedback. This is a proactive way to make your spreadsheets look professional and never reach one of those dreaded error values.

As a helpful note when setting this formula up on your spreadsheet, blank cells are evaluated as numeric cells.

Take a look at each of the options for the Type function in Excel 2013 below:

| Type Value | Description | Example |
|---|---|---|
| 1 | Numeric | 1337 |
| 2 | Text | I'm a Tiger! Rawr! |
| 4 | Logical Value | TRUE |
| 16 | Error Value | #N/A |
| 64 | Array | {0,1,2,3} |

How difficult is this function to use?

This function is complex to use by the nature of the additional setup it will take to utilize the integers returned in a meaningful way but the formula itself is actually quite easy to enter.

How do I use this function?

1. Open Microsoft Excel and locate the information that you wish to evaluate.

| | A | B |
|---|---|---|
| 1 | Number | 1337 |
| 2 | Text | I'm a Tiger! Rawr! |
| 3 | Logical Value | TRUE |
| 4 | Error Value | #N/A |
| 5 | Blank Cell | |
| 6 | Space Only | |

2. Activate the cell where you want to display the numeric result.

| | A | B | C |
|---|---|---|---|
| 1 | Number | 1337 | |
| 2 | Text | I'm a Tiger! Rawr! | |
| 3 | Logical Value | TRUE | |
| 4 | Error Value | #N/A | |
| 5 | Blank Cell | | |
| 6 | Space Only | | |

3. Type the Type function, "=TYPE(".

| | A | B | C |
|---|---|---|---|
| 1 | Number | 1337 | =TYPE( |
| 2 | Text | I'm a Tiger! Rawr! | TYPE(**value**) |
| 3 | Logical Value | TRUE | |
| 4 | Error Value | #N/A | |
| 5 | Blank Cell | | |
| 6 | Space Only | | |

4. Input your first (and only) argument, in this example "B1". This argument should be a reference to a cell. If you input a range, the result will always be an evaluation an error which is the value of "16".

| | A | B | C |
|---|---|---|---|
| 1 | Number | 1337 | =TYPE(B1 |
| 2 | Text | I'm a Tiger! Rawr! | TYPE(**value**) |
| 3 | Logical Value | TRUE | |
| 4 | Error Value | #N/A | |
| 5 | Blank Cell | | |
| 6 | Space Only | | |

51

5. Complete the function with a closing parenthesis ")".

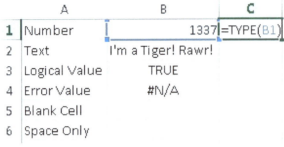

|   | A | B | C |
|---|---|---|---|
| 1 | Number | 1337 | =TYPE(B1) |
| 2 | Text | I'm a Tiger! Rawr! | |
| 3 | Logical Value | TRUE | |
| 4 | Error Value | #N/A | |
| 5 | Blank Cell | | |
| 6 | Space Only | | |

6. Hit "Enter".

|   | A | B | C |
|---|---|---|---|
| 1 | Number | 1337 | 1 |
| 2 | Text | I'm a Tiger! Rawr! | |
| 3 | Logical Value | TRUE | |
| 4 | Error Value | #N/A | |
| 5 | Blank Cell | | |
| 6 | Space Only | | |

7. Congratulations, you have now successfully used the Type function! The Type function will return a numeric value. Below is an example of what happens when you copy that formula down column C using the Fill Handle.

|   | A | B | C |
|---|---|---|---|
| 1 | Number | 1337 | 1 |
| 2 | Text | I'm a Tiger! Rawr! | 2 |
| 3 | Logical Value | TRUE | 4 |
| 4 | Error Value | #N/A | 16 |
| 5 | Blank Cell | | 1 |
| 6 | Space Only | | 2 |
| 7 | | | |

www.ingramcontent.com/pod-product-compliance
Lightning Source LLC
Chambersburg PA
CBHW041146050326
40689CB00001B/503